Old South Uist

Bill Innes

The ferry opened up easy access to Eriskay by car twenty years before it operated for the last time in July 2001 - on the day the new causeway was officially opened. Alasdair Morrison MSP, Calum MacDonald MP and Alex Macdonald, Convener of *Comhairle nan Eilean Siar*, disembark to meet the waiting press.

First Published in the United Kingdom, 2006
reprinted 2008
Stenlake Publishing Limited
54–58 Mill Square, Catrine, KA5 6RD
www.stenlake.co.uk

Printed by
Blissetts, Roslin Road, Acton, W3 8DH

ISBN 9781840333817

A two-horse gig waits in front of the Pollachar Inn circa 1905. Prior to the arrival of the causeway, the Uist terminal for Eriskay and Barra was at Ludag jetty. In olden times, the embarkation point had been at Pollachar. In the seventeenth century a change-house was set up there to meet the needs of ferry travellers. However, its exposed position at the southwest corner of the island and lack of a proper jetty made it an unreliable landing place.

Acknowledgements

Many people have assisted with pictures and information in the preparation of this little book. My thanks in particular to Magdalena Sagarzazu of the Canna Archive for permission to use some of Margaret Fay Shaw's classic photographs of the 1930s and Hugh Cheape of Scottish National Museums. Thanks also to Donald MacNeil of Comann Eachdraidh Uibhist a Deas for permission to use some of Kildonan Museum's archive. The museum will receive the royalties from this book.

Morag Cumming supplied pictures and details about her father, Donald Macintyre. Peter Bowie, (Howbeg), Neil Macmillan, (Milton), Ewen and Calum Laing, Peter Macintyre, (Furnace) and Helen MacDonald, (Teddington) were invaluable sources of information. My grateful thanks to all who put up with my queries.

This book is dedicated to the memory of Peter Bowie, Howbeg, 1923-2006

INTRODUCTION

In the mid 20th century (when women rarely ventured into pubs) the Pollachar Inn public bar would be the drinking place of choice for the men of the south end of the island, with the inns at Lochboisdale and Creagorry as the only competition. Calum Ewen Maclellan is seen enjoying a drink in the public bar circa 1980 when Donnie MacNeil was the proprietor.

"The natives speak the Irish tongue more perfectly here, than in most of the other islands; partly because of the remoteness and the small number of those that speak English, and partly because some of 'em are scholars and versed in the Irish language."

So wrote Skye man Martin Martin in the journal of his tour of the Hebrides at the end of the 17th Century. Sadly, in the early 21st century Gaelic is in as steady decline in the Uists as it is in other parts of the Highlands. The number of new learners is failing to match the decline in fluent speakers in either numbers or vocabulary while too many of the young (and their parents) have yet to realise that their language has acquired a new respect and status both nationally and internationally.

South Uist and Benbecula were part of the Clan Ranald lands till the middle of the 19th century. Thanks to the demand for kelp from seaweed at the turn of the 19th century, the chief prospered and the population soared to around 7300 to provide the necessary labour. After the Napoleonic wars the price of kelp collapsed due to competition from imported barilla and the chief soon found himself facing bankruptcy.

South Uist was sold to Lt. Col. John Gordon in 1837. His scant regard for his tenantry is demonstrated by his offer to the government that the islands would make a convenient penal colony. Emigration from Uist in the 18th century had been largely voluntary, especially in 1772 when 200 left for Prince Edward Island after MacDonald of Boisdale tried to compel his people to convert to the Protestant religion. But in 1849 and 1851, 2000 people were forcibly evicted and their homes burnt. They were taken to Quebec where they were abandoned without support. Families living on the east side behind the hills were also forcibly cleared to make way for sheep. Some were settled around Hartavagh Bay in the south east corner and then moved on to Eriskay which was deemed too exposed to be suitable for sheep and where the soil was unsuited to mechanical cultivation. The remaining population in South Uist was confined to the poor moorland of the central strip while the fertile machair land of the west was divided up into large tacks or farms. By 1861 the population had been reduced to 5,300.

There was little improvement when Colonel Gordon was succeeded by his daughter-in-law, Lady Gordon Cathcart. She was largely an absentee landlord and the people were still oppressed by her bailiffs. Another wave of emigration took place in 1883-4 – mainly to Saskatchewan. After the Napier Commission heard of the people's grievances, the Crofter's Act of 1886 gave security of tenure and in the first two decades of the 20th century crofters gained access to the machair land when most of the tacks were broken up. After the Great War, when jobs were scarce, there was further emigration in 1923 – mainly to Alberta.

Today the homes in South Uist are every bit as sophisticated as in any mainland community with broadband computer networks and satellite television, but before the latter half of the 20th century things were very different. Until mains water, electricity and the rocket range arrived in the mid 1950s, the arduous lifestyle of the crofter was one of subsistence through hard manual labour. Despite widespread poverty, there was a vibrant spirit of community cooperation and a richness of Gaelic oral culture which made the island a gold mine for folklore collectors. Irish folklore scholar James Delargy hailed this storehouse as one of the most important in western Europe.

That this oral culture survived for so long is at least partly due to the fact that the southern isles remained largely Catholic. Alexander Carmichael records in *Carmena Gadelica* that 19th century ministers and teachers in the more Calvinist islands dismissed music, dancing and story-telling as heathen frivolity. In South Uist and Barra there was neither education in Gaelic nor the Protestant emphasis on reading the Bible. As a result, few were literate in their own language. In compensation, many demonstrated extraordinary feats of memory in singing and story-telling. In the 1940s Calum Maclean (brother of Sorley) spent three years taking down stories from Angus Macmillan of Griminish. 10,000 pages of manuscript; 165 stories in all - of which forty-four were longer than three hours!

In 2006, South Uist entered a new and exciting phase as the community took over ownership of the estate.

The author in 1954 with a .22 rifle which served the useful function of producing food for the pot in addition to reducing raids on the crops. Rabbits were a welcome addition to the crofter's diet and their skins could be sold to travelling pedlars for a few shillings. In the 40s there was a fashion for hunting them at night by dazzling them with specially lengthened torches. This at least led to a swifter demise than the cruel gin traps.

Shortly after this snap was taken, the myxomatosis virus wreaked havoc and its distressing symptoms virtually eliminated rabbit from the menu.

Ged a gheibhinn-sa mo thagha, B' e mo rogha den Roinn Eòrpa
Aite-tuinidh 'n cois' na tuinne an Eilean grinn na h-òige…

If I were given my choice, I would pick of all Europe,
A dwelling by the waves in the lovely isle of youth…

So wrote Father Allan MacDonald who became parish priest at Eriskay in 1894 after ten years at St. Peter's in Daliburgh, South Uist. He was the prime mover behind the building of the church of St. Michael which dominates the Eriskay skyline. Famously the island fisherman promised to donate a night's catch towards the cost and the haul in question was a record one. Father Allan's memory is still revered in the islands not just as priest, but also as a bard and folklore collector. His collection of *Gaelic Words and Expressions from South Uist and Eriskay* (OUP 1972), edited by John Lorne Campbell, is an essential tool for any student of South Uist Gaelic. His Gaelic poetry and hymns have been published in books by John Lorne Campbell, *Bàrdachd Mhgr. Ailein* (Constable 1965) and Ronnie Black, *Eilean na h-Oige* (Mungo 2002) and his reputation attracted many visitors to the island. He was the model for the fictional Father Ludovic in Neil Munro's *Children of the Tempest*. Ada Goodrich Freer (next to him in the picture with her friend Constance and their dog 'Scamp') has been much criticised for using his folklore material without attribution for her own books and lectures. On the other hand her *Outer Isles* (William Constable 1902) makes it clear that she was moved and horrified by the oppression, misery and poverty she observed in South Uist under the absentee ownership of Lady Gordon Cathcart.

"There is, thank heaven, but one South Uist in the world, though in poverty, misery and neglect the island of Barra runs it very close… Nowhere in our proud empire is there a spot more desolate, grim, hopelessly poverty-stricken."

Father Allan died of pneumonia in 1905 at the tragically young age of 46 and has an imposing headstone in the old Eriskay cemetery. This 1898 picture was taken with the camera of Edinburgh publisher Walter Blaikie (far left) whose visit produced many other photographs of Eriskay.

© NTS MF Shaw Collection

Left to Right: Walter Blaikie, Miss Constance Moore, Ada Goodrich Freer, Fr. Allan MacDonald

© Kildonan museum

Seaweed has been of long term importance to the economy of the islands. The island population was at its highest when chiefs needed many hands to collect the kelp which was their principal source of income. The alkali ash was used in the manufacture of soap and glass. After the Second World War Alginate Industries (Scotland) Ltd. set up a factory at Boisdale to process the weed to a powder which had many uses, including food processing.

The rod-like tangle, *laminaria hyperborean*, was collected when it washed up on the shore after the winter storms and was air-dried on stands such as in the above picture before being processed. In 1952 there were 133 men employed in collecting seaweed in South Uist and Benbecula. But by the eighties cheaper sources of supply had been found and the factories at Boisdale and Sponish in North Uist closed down.

In the fifties thatched houses, such as these in South Boisdale, were still common on the island but the old order was changing rapidly as generous Department of Agriculture subsidies made it possible for crofters to build simple bungalows in the approved patterns.

By 1981 most of the thatched houses on the island had either been replaced or were falling into disrepair with weeds taking over the thatch as here in Smerclate. By contrast, the ultra- modern church at Garrynamonie can just be seen over the shoulder of the house on the left.

Facing the church (far left) can be seen the old school at Garrynamonie (now demolished) which figured in Frederick Rea's *A School in South Uist*.

In an island with very few trees, the thick layer of peat on the moorland was a vital fuel resource, available 'free' to the crofter - at the cost of much hard labour. Work on the peat was started after completion of spring ploughing and planting. First the top turf was stripped off and dumped in the previous year's ditch. The peat then revealed was usually dug by two man teams; the cutter using the *troighsgeir* (peat-spade) to lever out soggy, rectangular blocks which the thrower picked off the blade and chucked to one side or the other to begin the initial drying process.

Where the peat was deep enough, three spits could be taken out. Here we see three teams at work. If there was no extended family, neighbours helped each other in a spirit of mutual cooperation. In those days money rarely changed hands, but it was customary to provide a midday meal for the teams.

After three or four weeks, the peats were firm enough to be stood on end in *rùghain* - groups of three with a fourth placed on top. Eventually they were dry enough to be brought in sacks to a central point where they could be collected by cart or tractor. The aim was to have them built into a stack at home before the harvest workload started.

In an era when horses and cattle were much more numerous, the author's memory is that the labour-intensive nature of the operation was often made more tedious by plagues of flies and clegs. Whether or not the cleg's Sunday name of 'horsefly' is based on accurate scientific observation, the furtive little vampires seemed to delight in varying their diet with human blood.

©N.T.S. MF Shaw Collection

Seonaidh Campbell the bard, Donald Campbell, Aonghas Ruadh Campbell, Angus John Campbell and Donald John Campbell (nephews). Seated: James Campbell and Donald MacRae.

Gum b' inntinneach, togarrach obair na mònadh
A' direadh 's a' cromadh gun sìneadh do dhroma
'S an troighsgian a' sgonnadh nan golladan còsach…

Merry and uplifting the work on the peats,
Up and down without straining your back,
The foot-spade cleaving the fibrous peats…

Donald Macintyre

*'S a mhadainn choirb-fhuair le gaoith 's le stoirm
A bhith triall a dh'fheamnadh thug searbh-bhlas dhòmhs' air...*

Biting cold mornings with wind and storm
Soured my taste for collecting seaweed...

Donald John MacDonald

Bean Aonghais Ruadh, Mrs Angus Campbell of North Glendale brings seaweed for the fields. Seaweed was an invaluable natural fertiliser, supplementing manure from cattle and horses. Apart from commercial processing (q.v.) the weed was gathered in early spring (often in inclement weather as the bard ruefully reflects) and left in heaps to rot down before being spread on the fields. It was particularly useful on the machair where it helped to add body to the sandy soil. After the winter storms there was often a plentiful supply washed up on the west coast beaches, but on the rockier east coast it was usually necessary to cut weed from the rocks at low tide. When kelp was an important commercial crop for the landlords in the nineteenth century, the people were often banned from "wasting" this natural resource to enrich their smallholdings.

A pony with a balanced pair of creels could be used in terrain unsuitable for carts and was for a woman or adolescent easier to manage than a heavy cart. Those who did not have a pony had to carry a single creel on their backs.

John Morrison, *Iagan Raghaill*, of South Lochboisdale demonstrates the use of the *caschrom* in the 1930s. The level fields of the western machairs made for ideal ploughing territory but most of the best arable land was allocated to tacksmen until the beginning of the 20th century. On soggy moorland and the rockier east coast there were few areas suitable for ploughing, so much cultivation was perforce by spade and *caschrom* (foot–plough). These basic tools made it possible for the subsistence crofter to utilise every scrap of available land for potatoes, rotated with barley or oats.

The English translation of *feannagan* as 'lazy-beds' does grave injustice to the amount of work involved. Strips of land three to five feet wide were marked out and the turf between cut vertically with a conventional spade. After seaweed or manure fertiliser had been applied, the seed potatoes could either be laid directly on the surface or inserted later by dibber. The foot-plough was then used (working backwards) to turn over the first sod, *ploc-mala*, onto each side of the central strip. The resulting furrow between the strips was further excavated (*taomadh*) to cover the remaining central space. The strips ran down-slope so the end result not only raised the seed bed but further improved drainage via the intermediate ditches. The furrowed traces of old *feannagan* can still be seen, often in some very inhospitable and tiny spots.

© NTS/MF Shaw Collection

This photograph illustrates all too vividly the back-breaking drudgery of cutting corn by sickle. The scythe (q.v.) by comparison was quicker, easier and much more efficient. However, the sickle was widely used until the thirties.

Peigi and Mairi MacRae in North Glendale came originally from North Uist and were cousins of Donald Ferguson who owned the big house and shop in South Lochboisdale. It was there that folklore collector Margaret Fay Shaw heard them sing and they became her hosts during her time in Uist in the nineteen thirties. They provided over fifty of the songs she published in the landmark *Folksongs and Folklore of South Uist*. In total she recorded 270 songs from Peigi – particularly after electric recorders became available. As noted in the introduction, such feats of memory were not unusual among island singers and storytellers.

The sisters' hospitality played a large part in the strong affection for South Uist and its people that Margaret Fay Shaw maintained until her dying day in 2004 at the age of 101.

Ian Campbell, *Iain mac Dhòmhnaill 'ic Iain Bhàin*, was a member of a well-known South Lochboisdale traditional bardic family. His trade of stone-mason involved him in building hotels in Oban and the church in Castlebay as well as many houses in his own island.

His sons carried on the bardic tradition. Roderick (*Ròidseag*) in particular is remembered for one of Gaelic's best known love songs – *A Pheigi a Ghràidh*. Ian's brother *Seonaidh* was another prolific bard. John MacInnes, *Iain Pheadair*, (q.v.) collected over a hundred songs from him. Forty eight of them were published by John Lorne Campbell as *Orain Ghàidhlig Sheonaidh Caimbeul* (JB Mackay 1936).

Here, Ian is winding the heather rope which was widely used to secure thatch and corn stacks. For less demanding, temporary applications a less robust rope could be wound from marram grass, corn straw or hay. A handful of hens (standard for most households before the arrival of mink) scratch an organic livelihood in the background. Note the metal wind-protecting cap on the trademark pipe. Well-stoked with strong-smelling Black Twist, such were the standard companions of many men of the time.

© Bill Innes

South Lochboisdale was so noted for its poets that it is known as *Gleann na Ceòlraidh*, Glen of the Muses. Donald MacDonald, *Dòmhnall Aonghais Bhàin* was perhaps the last of a long roll of honour of Uist traditional bards. Like so many others, he did not live to see his work published in book form. *Smuaintean fo Eiseabhal* (Birlinn, edited by Ronnie Black) was launched posthumously in 2000 at an event graced by the presence of Margaret Fay Shaw.

Donald's thatched house was one of the last in Uist to be maintained in its original form. The basic format was of three rooms with kitchen and main bedroom separated by a smaller bedroom (or *clòsaid*) which shared the middle of the house with a short passage from front door to kitchen. Note that in South Uist thatch was taken to the edge of the outer wall, whereas in some other islands there was a ledge round the periphery.

© Bill Innes

In the internal picture can be seen a typical example of the peat-burning stoves which were such a huge advance when they replaced open fire and *slabhraidh* (pot-hanging chain). The stove not only provided an oven for baking and four cooking rings, but also ensured that much more of the heat stayed within the house rather than vanishing up the chimney. A line under the mantelpiece provided a quick-drying facility for socks and other small items.

The standard furniture of the kitchen usually consisted of a long bench under the window, dresser and meal-chest against the far wall, table against the partition wall and a few chairs.

The Bute hospital in Daliburgh was founded in 1894, thanks to the generosity of the Marchioness of Bute who continued to support it. It was staffed by nuns from the Order of the Sacred Heart, but was open to all. Although it had only fourteen beds, it is recorded that in 1899 (at the time of a severe typhus outbreak) there were sixty-six patients.

Before it was replaced by the expensive new Benbecula hospital in 2002, a considerable amount of routine surgery was carried out there by island doctors and visiting surgeons. The new hospital has a state-of-the-art operating theatre but ironically it often lies unused due to the more stringent levels of experience now demanded of operating staff. The old building has a new lease of life as a Care Centre for old people.

This 1936 view across *Loch nan Clachan Mòra* in Daliburgh shows the wide spread of water lilies which ornament many Uist lochs in summer. They are also visible in the next picture which shows the same loch from the reverse viewpoint.

This 1965 picture taken from the old Post Office shows (centre) the corrugated iron structure which was Daliburgh Higher Grade school. It contained three classrooms – one for each of the first three years of Secondary school. Despite a complete lack of resources by today's standards, Latin and Shakespeare were staple items in the curriculum from First Year on. How many of the huge secondary schools of today could claim as much? Eventually a more modern building was opened half a mile further south, but the secondary pupils of today are educated in the splendidly equipped school at Liniclate, Benbecula.

Far left is the house of Alan MacDonald, whose shop, *Bùth Ailein Mhòir*, was in the extension to the right of the house. Competition was provided by the Cooperative which occupied the shed seen on the far right of the school. Together with George Macmillan's little general shop (*Bùth Sheòrais Nill*) halfway along the Daliburgh road, these were the main shops in the village in the post-war period. Island shops in general were often just annexes to the owner's house but were expected to stock general crofting hardware as well as basic foodstuffs. These latter arrived in bulk; tea from chests was weighed carefully into coarse brown paper bags, cheese and bacon hand-sliced by wire and machine respectively.

Daliburgh Higher Grade School
c. 1928

Back Row: Archie MacRury, Stoneybridge; Donald MacDonald; Donald Archie MacDonald, Benbecula; ? Macaulay; Donald Eoin MacDonald, Peninerine; Hector Maclean, Nunton (later Church of Scotland minister).

Middle Row: Miss Robb, teacher; Fred Morrison, Gerinish; Christine Macphee (Mackay), Eochar; Mary Mackinnon, Strome; Jessie Macintyre (Macaulay), Garrynamonie; Annie Macleod, Daliburgh; Catherine MacQueen, Eochar; Angus Campbell, S. Lochboisdale; Alick Fraser, teacher.

Front Row: William Lomax, (son of headmaster); Mary Kate MacDonald (Macphee); Joan Morrison; Fred Lomax, headmaster; Katie Mackay; Mary Macaulay, Daliburgh; Mary Morrison (Macintyre), Kilphedar; Alasdair Maclean (policeman's son).

Sitting on ground: Bernard Flynn, Eriskay; Robert Maclean, Daliburgh; John Walker, Bornish.

This was a most distinguished group, many of whom went on to successful careers. John Walker (who was an invaluable source of information) retired in Campbeltown, where he had been headmaster. The legendary Fred Lomax was still the headmaster when the author attended Daliburgh in the late forties. Robert Maclean was the first Uist man to lose his life in the war and Archie MacRury was also killed in action as a tail gunner in the RAF. Donald Eoin Macdonald (brother of bard Donald John Macdonald) was a brilliant scholar whose potential was cruelly blighted when he contracted TB while at school in Fort William. He died in 1934 aged 21. Donald MacDonald, Eriskay, was crowned bard at the 1949 National Mod in Inverness. Fred Morrison was a piper and headmaster. Christine Macphee became a teacher and a bard. She married Alec Mackay, headmaster of Garrynamonie school. Jessie Macintyre (Macaulay), Annie Macleod and Catherine Macqueen also became teachers. Mary Kate MacDonald was a half-sister of the bard Donald Allan MacDonald. Joan Morrison was a sister of Canon John Morrison, who famously resisted the establishment of the rocket range in his parish and was the moving force behind the erection of the statue at Rueval.

© Bill Innes

St. Peter's, Daliburgh, (built in 1868) is the parish church for the south end of the island. The population of South Uist is mainly Catholic although there is a happy co-existence with the substantial Protestant minority.

In the 1950s the strong faith of the Catholic congregations found public expression in processions to open-air services. Such a procession is seen leaving St Peter's, in 1957. In those days the sexes were segregated in church; it can be seen that the women are only just emerging to join the back of the procession.

© Bill Innes

Roderick MacDonald, *Ruaridh Posta* had the task of delivering the mails from Lochboisdale to the other post offices in the island. Initially this was done on horseback or by cart, but by 1922 he had acquired a left hand drive model T Ford – one of the first cars on the island. His passenger is Ian Macphee, *Iain Saor*, from Frobost.

The last major wave of emigration was in 1923 when the *Marloch* collected emigrants from several islands. At over 10,000 tons she was too large to moor at Lochboisdale so the passengers were transferred by smaller ships. The tender at the pier in this poignant picture of leave-taking looks like the McCallum Orme ship *Hebrides* - a regular visitor to the islands at the time.

The eventual destination of many of these Uist migrants was a community named Clandonald, some 160 miles east of Edmonton, Alberta. Sadly, many of them were not much better off for they found themselves on poor, uncleared land for which they had to pay up to a third of their annual yield as rent to the Canadian Pacific Railway.

L to R: Mrs Maclellan, *Bean Iagain Chaluim*, Mrs Macleod, *Bean Eoghain 'ic Iagain*, Mrs MacDonald, *Bean Ruaridh Phosta*, (in hat), Mrs Buchanan, *Sorcha Illeasbaig Gobha*, Fr. Joseph Gillies, Betty MacFarlane, Johnathan Macintyre, *Eòin Mac Iain Mhòir*, South Boisdale, emigrating to join his sons.

This picture was taken on the day that the emigrants had to leave their native isle for Canada. Father Gillies was a Barra man and the ladies are from Lochboisdale with the exception of Mrs Buchanan from Strome and Betty Macfarlane from Caolas Stulaidh (her father was a shepherd on the east side of the island). A white shawl was a common headdress for a married woman; widows wore a black version.

The coaster *Halcyon* lies at the Lochboisdale pier long before the link span was added to accommodate the Ro-Ro ferries. A couple of fishing boats are moored behind. In the 1940s and 1950s, the large building to the left contained the two main shops of Fred Gillies and Johnny Clark.

The pipe band of the 4th/5th Cameron Highlanders plays in front of the Lochboisdale Hotel in the late 1950s. Leading the band is Drum Major William Urquhart from Nairn while the Pipe Major (piper nearest the camera) is Neil Macmillan from Milton. South Uist has long been famous for its pipers. Those in the band at the time included William Mackillop from Lochcarnan and Alasdair J. Campbell from Kildonan.

Behind the band is the David MacBrayne bus which provided such a vital service in the days before mass car ownership and in the background is the Lochboisdale Hotel whose proprietor, the larger-than-life Finlay Mackenzie, had himself served in the 4th Camerons as a young man.

In the post-war days, Lochboisdale was the most important focus of island social life. As most passengers departed and arrived on foot, the pier would be thronged three nights a week with people meeting and greeting the connecting ferries *Lochearn* and *Lochmor* from Oban and Mallaig respectively. The hotel has always been a haunt of anglers and sportsmen but on ferry nights this business was supplemented by a roaring men-only trade in the bars. At the time, women rarely entered public bars.

The pier area also boasted the two general merchant shops of Johnny Clark and Fred Gillies, mentioned opposite.
The arrival of Ro-Ro ferries was to have a major impact on Lochboisdale's economy as passengers could drive straight to or from their destinations without any need to spend time in the port.

This group photograph (probably taken at the South Uist Games circa 1955) includes two of South Uist's best known 20th century tradition bearers. Second left at the back (wearing the dark hat) is Angus Maclellan, *Aonghas Beag mac Aonghais 'ic Eachainn*, (1869-1966). Thanks to John Lorne Campbell, his traditional tales and reminiscences of his working life have been preserved in *Stories from South Uist* and *The Furrow Behind Me* (both reprinted by Birlinn). The Gaelic original of the latter volume, *Saoghal an Treobhaiche*, is a splendid storehouse of colloquial Uist language and Angus was awarded an MBE in recognition of his contribution to the preservation of island folklore.

Sitting next to him in the picture (grey hat) is Donald Macintyre, *Dòmhnall Ruadh Phàislig*, (1889-1964) - another master of language and one of the finest Gaelic traditional poets of the 20th (or any other) century. His great masterpiece, *Aeòlus agus am Balg*, won him the Bardic crown at the National Mod in Glasgow in 1938 and his poetry was published posthumously in *Sporan Dhòmhnaill*, (Scottish Gaelic Texts Society 1968). He is commemorated on a monument by the side of the road near his birthplace in Snishival. His wife Mary is at the front of the group on the left with their son Angus immediately behind her. The young man top left is John Cumming and to the right of Donald is his wife's brother Donald Maclellan, *Dòmhnall Beag 'ille Bhrìde*, and niece Kate, *Ceiteig Flòraidh*, who was married to another famous Uist bard, Donald Alan MacDonald, *Dòmhnall Ailean Dhòmhnaill na Bainich*.

© Morag Cumming

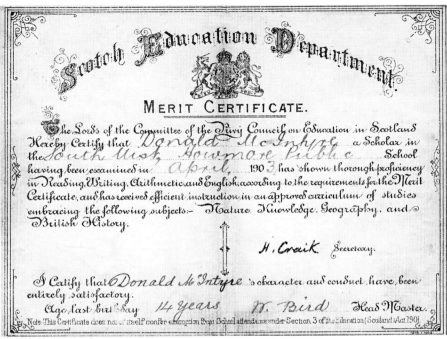

© Morag Cumming

In this picture from the 1950s, Donald Macintyre is seen with his son Angus after a successful day's fishing. Most of South Uist's fishing is controlled but it can be seen from the improvised nature of the rod that this day of sport was unlikely to have been officially sanctioned! Donald was merely maintaining the poaching traditions of his childhood which he described in the nostalgic poem *Sùil air Ais*.

Bhiodh abhainn air a tàbhach,	The river would be netted,
Is cabhuil air gach àthan,	Fish traps on every ford,
Is Sasannaich a' cnàmhan	While Englishmen complained,
Nach tàrradh iad lann!	Not a scale could they catch!

Although the use of the word 'Scotch' for anything other than whisky is sneered at nowadays, note that it was apparently quite acceptable to the Education Department in 1903. Like many other intelligent islanders, Donald had to leave school at 14, despite his obvious academic ability – a school inspector is reported to have said, 'That little red-haired boy could be Chancellor of the Exchequer!'

His certificate testifies to the wide range of subjects taught at the little two-room school at Howmore at the beginning of the 20th century. The conspicuous exception is Gaelic. Island children of the time would be monoglot Gaelic speakers before going to school, but their teacher, Winifred Bird, was English (as was Frederick Rea who wrote of his contemporaneous experiences in *A School in South Uist*).

Above: This 1895 picture shows the market stance to the west of the main road at Loch Ollaidh, which was still marked on Ordnance Survey maps long after it fell out of use in the 1920s. The annual market in September was the main opportunity to sell cattle and horses, but it also became a major social occasion attended by stallholders, travelling people and pedlars as well as drovers and islanders from all levels of society. The presence of whisky tents made for some rowdy scenes but Frederick Rea also records that stalls selling sweets did a roaring trade with customers of all ages. Eventually auction sales of stock at venues such as Rueval, Stoneybridge and Carrisaval replaced the central market.

Right: Roddy Macphee of Ormiclate and Peter Bowie building a corn stack from sheaves in the traditional way to provide winter feed for the cattle. The stack tapered to a conical top and would be secured with tarpaulin and/or coir ropes weighted with stones against the winter gales.

© Bill Innes

A bhliadhna chun an aimsir seo, b' fhoirmeil sinn an Ormacleit,
An cùirt an leoghainn mheargasaich, gu fearghalach, neo mhordhalach –

Just a year ago – what pomp we had in Ormiclate,
At the court of the fiery lion, virile without arrogance –

The ruins of the castle still dominate the Ormiclate skyline, yet its period of pomp was extremely brief. Young Allan MacDonald, Captain of Clanranald (*Ailean Dearg*) had a distinguished military career fighting on the French side in the Spanish wars of succession. In Spain he met and married Penelope Mackenzie, daughter of the governor of Tangiers, and brought her home to South Uist. She is reported to have scorned his then residence as 'no better than her father's henhouse' so Allan brought masons and stone from France to build her a new home – more chateau than castle. After seven years in the building, it was completed in 1708.

Seven years later, Allan was killed at the battle of Sheriffmuir and tradition has it that the castle burned down accidentally the same night while a deer was being roasted in the kitchen for an unofficial servant's party. If it is true that the fire was accidental, then it is a strange coincidence. It is known that, prior to Sheriffmuir, Allan had ordered the deliberate burning of the clan's key stronghold, Castle Tioram in Moidart, lest it fall into enemy hands. The odds must be high against such a conjunction of events being accidental. While it seems unlikely that he would have believed Ormiclate to be threatened, it is known that he had a presentiment that he would not return. (Some notes of Donald John MacDonald suggest an alternative theory that the castle was deliberately destroyed as punishment for the young chief's part in the uprising).

On Allan Macdonald's death the estate passed to his brother Ranald who died in 1725 – also without heir – and then to Donald MacDonald of Benbecula who was married to their sister Janet. Thus the clan seat moved to Nunton House in Benbecula.

© Bill Innes

Apart from the men's fashions, this 1985 picture taken at Ormiclate has a timeless quality in that the collection of sheep for shearing by hand has been going on for generations. Sheep spent the summer out on the hills while the croft lands were cultivated. For all their sedate image, they often displayed a fearless agility on challenging slopes. On the appointed day (usually in July) men and dogs gathered for the community exercise of collecting them to the township fank. A sheep's owner was identified by coloured keel marks on its wool, brands on its horns and patterns of slits and cuts in its ears. However, shepherds recognised individual sheep by their facial features, which are just as unique as those of humans.

After hand-shearing came the indignity of total immersion in a tank of strong-smelling dip to protect against parasites. That was nothing to the indignity inflicted on the male lambs – save for the few deemed worthy of being future rams! Eventually the newly shorn and dipped flocks were returned to the hill.

© George Johnstone

© George Johnstone

Below: Ronald Johnstone (*Raghall Og Mac Dhonnchaidh 'ac Lachlainn*) of Ormiclate is seen here with the stallion provided by the Board of Agriculture. Although bulls were provided for each township, there might be only one stallion for the whole island. However large his area of responsibility, the keeper was not allowed to ride – for the stallion's stamina had to be conserved. The only burden permitted (as seen here) was a bag of feed – and the keeper's coat! It follows that the amount of walking involved was considerable but this was not deemed unusual in an era when few people had cars and most walked everywhere.

Above: Ronald Johnstone (*Raghall Mòr mac Dhonnchaidh 'ac Lachlainn*) of Howbeg with his two horses in the early 1950s. Although one was sufficient for drawing the standard crofter's cart, two were necessary for the single furrow plough. As can be seen, the horses were small but sturdy animals. Their workload started in the early spring with collecting seaweed from the shore for use as fertiliser and continued through the cycle of ploughing, harrowing and collecting peats from the moor until the hay and corn harvest was brought in. Part of that harvest was required to feed them throughout the dark days of winter for, unlike tractors, horses need to be fed whether they are working or not.

Ronald was the elder brother of the other Ronald Johnstone shown with the stallion in the other picture. The island protocol of naming children after their forebears often resulted in duplication. Brothers in Uist were usually distinguished by adjectives such as *mòr* (big) and *beag* (small) or, as in this case, *òg* (young). In Lewis the necessary differentiation was often achieved by the use of nicknames.

© Bill Innes

Left: In the 1950s every croft had a handful of cows which were a key part of the island economy. Many of them were hardy Highlanders with a liberal sprinkling of Shorthorn and Ayrshires crosses. In the general absence of croft fences at the time, the task of keeping stock away from cultivated fields was usually delegated to the children. The milk provided butter and cheese and the stirks were sold to mainland drovers at the annual sales – often at pathetically low prices.

The Department of Agriculture provided each township with a good quality bull. Despite the fearsome sweep of their horns, these Highland bulls were gentle creatures. In fact, cross-bred cows could be more treacherous – as the author discovered to his cost in childhood! Responsibility for the bull's upkeep was shared out between the crofts and a little byre was set aside in each township for over-wintering. Later on, however, bulls were returned to the mainland for over-wintering.

© Bill Innes

Right: There was a long tradition of riding horses in the Uists – as Martin Martin observed in his *Description of the Western Isles of Scotland* at the end of the 17th century. In North Uist he recorded that horse-racing on Michaelmas day was a popular event attended by both sexes.

"The manner of running is by a few young men, who use neither saddles nor bridles except two small ropes made of bent instead of a bridle…"

In South Uist, "I perceived about sixty horsemen riding along the sands…"

The last great horse race in South Uist is reported to have been in 1820 and the use of horses for sport faded further when the estates were sold to Colonel Gordon circa 1840. From then on, survival became the main priority for the average crofter. However, island men made valuable recruits for the horse–mounted Lovat Scouts in the Second World War.

It can be seen that in the 1950s horses were still being ridden without need for saddle or stirrups. In the author's childhood, opportunities were rare as the horse's energy was too important a resource to be squandered unnecessarily. However, in spring the plough could be left on the machair while the ploughman rode home.

There is evidence of transition in this 1957 picture. The Howbeg road is still un-metalled and the outhouses are still thatched. Top centre is the stable – which had once been the Bowie house. Immediately beneath it is the roof of a byre for three cows. The larger building, top right, is the barn which still has a chimney for the kiln where oats and barley could be dried prior to milling. To its left is the cart. The yard between the outhouses was once the stack yard, but the area left of picture was easier of access for tractors. Marching through the whole picture are the poles and wires of the new mains electricity which revolutionised the Uist lifestyle.

Donald John MacDonald (1919 - 86), of Peninerine was another of South Uist's famous poets, winning the bardic crown at the National Mod in Glasgow in 1948. A self-educated man, his true importance as poet and philosopher was not fully appreciated until his collected works appeared posthumously in *Chì Mi*, I See, (Birlinn 2001). His other works included *Fo Sgàil a' Swastika*, Under the Shadow of the Swastika, (Acair 2000) a gripping account in parallel translation of his five years as a prisoner of war. The English version formed part of *St Valery: the Impossible Odds* (Birlinn 2004).

He also did invaluable work as a folklore collector and the School of Scottish Studies holds some 6000 pages of material handwritten by him.

In the picture he is accompanied by his wife Nellie at the Gaelic Books Council van with which Director of the Council, Ian MacDonald, used to tour the islands. Donald John is commemorated jointly with his uncle Donald Macintyre (q.v.) by a cairn beside the A865 at Snishival.

The old school at the Howmore crossroads had a later reincarnation as a guesthouse. In its heyday it had only two rooms. The top primary classes occupied the larger room while the entry classes were introduced to the alien language of English in the other.

In the author's childhood slates were still being used for routine work, while joined up writing was painstakingly practised against the impossibly perfect examples in copybooks. Children using steel nib pens sat in desks facing forward. The ink in the wells in the desk was mixed from powder by some of the more trustworthy bigger boys. A cupboard in the corner contained all the books available and enjoyed the rather grand title of 'The Library'.

At the age of ten or eleven, the Bursary exam could be taken which allowed the brighter to progress to secondary education at Daliburgh. (q.v.) However, many of the children were required for the heavy manual work of the croft and stayed on reluctantly till the minimum leaving age of fourteen. The bard Donald John MacDonald, despite his intelligence, was one of those desperate to leave as soon as possible.

Bha sgoil Hogh Mòir na chuis ghràin leinn
'S chan fhaighte leisgeul ga fàgail;
Bu tric a theich sinn a Hàrsal
'S a-mach gu h-àrd os a cionn.

Howmore school we detested
But had no excuse to leave;
We often bunked off to Haarsal
And to the heights beyond.

Donald John MacDonald

Howmore School 1936
Back Row: Alan Macleod, Ann MacDonald, Dolina Mackinnon, Peggy Stewart, Peter Bowie
2nd Back Row: Katie Dingwall, Mary Stewart, Lilian Macleod, Flora Morrison, Mary Dingwall, Mary Flora MacNeil, Ann Haggerty, Anna Laing
2nd Front Row: Willie Dingwall, Alasdair MacDonald, Alasdair MacEachan, Duncan Mackinnon, Ewen Dingwall(?), Duncan Bowie, Lachlan Macleod, John Mackinnon
Front Row: Donald Maclean, Ewen Laing, Archie Mackinnon, Donald John MacEachan, John Macleod.

© Bill Innes

Many Uist lochs have the ruins of ancient forts on tiny islets approached by stepping stones. Beagram on Loch an Eilein in Drimsdale is the best preserved. Once a much taller structure, it is recorded as being occupied in the seventeenth century.

The dominating structure in the background is Howmore Church of Scotland (q.v.). The thatched house to its left has survived into the 21st century as a youth hostel. Far left are the ruins of the various chapels which constitute the most important religious site on the island. It is believed that there was once a seminary here – part of the see of Iona. The importance of the old graveyard is underlined by the fact that it was once the burial place of Clan Ranald chiefs.

Reverend Malcolm Laing (1888 - 1968) was minister of Howmore Church of Scotland for twenty one years from 1926 till 1947. He married local girl Mary MacRury and also served the island as a JP. In all he was fifty years in the ministry, finally retiring in Alness in the year before his death.

In this picture from 1936 he is accompanied by his young son, Ewen. The venue is the livestock sale which used to be held at Rueval, east of the main road at Gerinish. On the right is James Shearer, manager of the Commercial Bank in Lochboisdale. It was customary for the bank manager to attend sales in order to handle cash transactions for animals sold.

Howmore church was built in 1854 to a design by Archibald Scott of Edinburgh. It is one of the very few in Scotland which retain a central communion table. There are at least two other examples - the churches at Croic (where victims of the Sutherland clearances sought refuge) and Achanaba by Loch Etive.

© Bill Innes

Donald Mackay of Howmore was one of the last to continue with the old manual methods of cultivation. The Y-handled scythe (*speal beag*) he is seen using in 1988 was more popular in Uist than the *speal mòr* which had both handles on one curved stem. Although the basic design dates back to the 18th century it did not totally supplant the sickle (q.v.) in Uist until well into the 20th. Even then, it was considered exotic enough to be known as the '*Ban-Shasannach*' – 'The Englishwoman'!

Until the 1950s the rasp of scythes being sharpened by whetstone resounded throughout the machair in autumn. There was an art to using a scythe. The best practitioners moved with a steady rhythm, leaving the stubble absolutely even. They also cut much shorter than any machine – thus extracting more of the vital foodstuff. The scythe was particularly useful where bad weather had flattened part of the crop.

It was part of the art of cutting corn that individual stems should fall neatly in parallel thus making life easier for the other member of the team who had to bind the sheaves by hand. This last chore involved a back-breaking amount of bending, so the author was particularly delighted when he eventually achieved a sufficient level of expertise to be trusted with the cutting part of the operation. The bound sheaves were arranged in stooks of six or eight until they were dry enough to be piled in small ricks. Eventually they were brought home by cart or tractor to be built into larger stacks, well secured with ropes and stones against winter storms.

© Bill Innes

© Bill Innes

After the defeat at Culloden in 1746, Prince Charles Edward Stuart famously took refuge in the Western Isles. Despite the bounty of £30,000 on his head he was never betrayed to the pursuing forces of the Crown. He spent some time on the east side of South Uist in a hunting lodge of Clan Ranald before escaping to Skye disguised as an Irish maid of the legendary Flora MacDonald and accompanied by the faithful John MacEachen of Howbeg. At the time the area behind the Uist hills had many crofting families, but they were later to be ruthlessly evicted to make way for sheep.

The Ordnance Survey map of South Uist shows 'Prince Charlie's Cave' in the south flank of Cas fo Thuath – the northern ridge descending east of Ben Corodale. This cave is shallow and open and would have been quite useless as a hiding place. However, there is a much more suitable hidden cave on the northeast shoulder of the southern ridge, Cas fo Dheas. The author's son, Stuart, is seen in 1995 by the tiny entrance which is made all the more difficult to spot by summer bracken. It opens up to a subterranean chamber which would have been a perfect temporary hiding place.

South Uist has no harbours on the exposed western coast but Lochboisdale, Locheynort and Lochskipport have all been important at different periods. Locheynort would have been used when the chief's residence was at Ormiclate and the ruins of the first inn can still be seen at *Airigh nam Ban*.

Lochskipport has a very sheltered harbour and it was provided with a pier in 1879 by Lady Gordon Cathcart. This uncharacteristic bout of generosity may have some connection with the fact that the residence of owners of the island was now at the adjacent Grogarry Lodge. She is also credited with planting the rare grove of trees and bushes seen on the road to the pier.

Lochskipport became an important port of call for the cargo ships such as *Dunara Castle*, *Hebrides* and *Clydesdale* which departed Glasgow to spend a week meandering round the islands. The first two had long been part of the McCallum Orme fleet until it was taken over by David MacBrayne in 1948.

The family of Malcolm Macleod, *Calum a' Mhuilich*, traded from Lochskipport, supplying the middle district with groceries and general merchandise by van. They eventually took over the post office at Stilligarry.

Lochard was the last of the dedicated cargo vessels to be built for MacBrayne, entering service in 1955. The advent of Ro-ro ferries allowed heavy lorries access to the narrow island roads, eventually rendering the more specialised vessels redundant. Lochskipport pier has long fallen into disrepair.

Nowadays the Cattle Show takes place at Eochar towards the end of July but in 1936 the venue was east of the main road at Gerinish. Ponies and Highland cattle would have been among the strongest categories and the prize giving would probably have been at the old Gerinish School (since demolished).

Mrs Flora Johnstone is seen with her dog at her cottage in Eochar. Its seashell-covered walls made it something of a tourist attraction in its day, particularly as a similar decoration scheme had been applied to an old bus parked behind which served as her greenhouse. After her death, both fell into disrepair.

In older pictures it can be seen that many ropes (usually of heather) were needed to secure the thatch. The arrival of wire netting considerably simplified the task. In this picture the zigzag pattern of brown coir rope linking the sheets can be seen. The same rope was also used to attach the stones which weighted the netting down against the winter gales.

Work on the South Ford bridge started in 1938 and it was eventually completed in 1941, bringing to an end the perilous gamble with the tides that crossing the ford to Benbecula had entailed. It was known locally as the 'O'Regan Bridge' because Fr. Patrick O'Regan of St. Mary's, Benbecula had been the very active president of a committee agitating for a bridge before the war. However, its wartime building was undoubtedly given added priority by the need to access the Coastal Command aerodrome at Balivanich. Its single carriageway with passing places soon became inadequate for the extra traffic generated by the rocket range so it was eventually replaced by a two lane causeway in 1982.

As can be seen, the old bridge allowed free passage to the fast-flowing island tides. The new solid causeway, however, formed an obstruction which islanders believe contributed to the flooding which so tragically claimed five lives from an island family in the storm of January 2005.

© Bill Innes

The sands of the ford have long been famous for their cockles which provided a welcome addition to the island diet. In the late 1950s, Tony Innes, Roderick Bowie and Donald John MacNeil pass a Sunday afternoon in a little gentle exploitation of this natural resource. They are armed only with spoons rather than the rakes of the commercial diggers – and the work is not allowed to interrupt the inevitable cigarette smoking of the time!

In this picture the sands of the ford would seem to provide an easy passage but conditions could change very rapidly with the tides (as many travellers found to their cost).

Left: Nowadays the Uists are part of the Eileanan Siar with the seat of local government in Stornoway. This picture records the last meeting of the South Uist District Council in May 1975.

Eriskay schoolmaster Donald MacDonald was crowned Bard at the 1949 National Mod in Inverness (see also the 1928 Daliburgh school photograph).

John MacInnes, *Iain Pheadair*, from South Lochboisdale was a legend in his own lifetime. In the 1940s and 1950s he was the entire social services for the islands of South Uist, Benbecula and Eriskay. It was said that when he retired it took six to replace him – a number that has increased considerably since! As singer, raconteur and local historian, his voice is still heard in recordings on Radio nan Gaidheal.

Charles Cameron (younger son of Locheil) was director of Alginate Industries (Scotland) Ltd which ran the Uist seaweed factories.

Standing L to R: Mr Donald A. Macaulay, Fr. MacNeil, Donald MacDonald.
Seated L to R: Donald Macleod (clerk), John MacInnes, Charles Cameron.

Right: Given the Highland chiefs' practice of building castles on the shore where normal access would be by galley, it may seem strange that the ruins of Borve Castle stand in a level field some distance from the sea. In fact the castle provides vivid evidence of the impact of shifting sands on the island coastline. It is believed to have been built in the middle of the 14th century by Aimi MacRuari and at that time stood on a rocky islet. Certainly the other great castle she built – Castle Tioram in Moidart – is a classic example of using such a site for defensive purposes.

Aimi was the first wife of her cousin John of Islay, Lord of the Isles. Despite the fact that she brought to the marriage a massive estate stretching from Moidart to the Uists, he divorced her in order to make an even more politically advantageous marriage to Margaret, daughter of Robert II of Scotland. Aimi is credited with building several island churches as well as the strategic castles.

The author's eleven year old son atop the castle wall gives scale to this picture taken in 1981. Sadly, Borve has crumbled even more since then, so attempts to follow his example should be strongly discouraged.

Above: The Creagorry Inn dates from 1885. Its original proprietor was James Bain, a builder from Ayrshire who came to Uist to build schools after the 1872 Education Act. Bain is also credited with bringing a Clydesdale stallion which was to have a beneficial influence on the sturdiness and stature of the local bloodstock.

The Macaulay family took over in 1920 and the Creagorry bar became the preferred drinking spot for the men in the north end of Uist as well as Benbecula – particularly at the time of the building of Benbecula Aerodrome and the South Ford bridge. It has now been completely refurbished in its new incarnation as the Isle of Benbecula House Hotel.

Left: Mrs Macaulay of the Creagorry Inn is seen with the vehicle that ferried passengers across the fords.

© Bill Innes

Aviation became accepted in the islands long before it became routine on the mainland. In the 1930s mainline trains were more reliable and sometimes faster than the flimsy aircraft of the time. However, the journey from Glasgow to the islands might take two days by surface transport, so a two hour flight had obvious attractions.

Early pioneers like David Barclay started commercial air services to the Western Isles in 1935 via Glen Brittle in Skye. Initially the landing places were on the machair at Askernish and Sollas for South and North Uist respectively. Benbecula was added later but eventually became the preferred site for the war-time Coastal Command airfield. From 1933 on, the aeroplane served also as an ambulance - giving the sick speedy access to city hospitals and thereby saving hundreds of lives.

In 1946 the various small airlines of Scotland were amalgamated under the umbrella of British European Airways, which in turn merged with British Overseas Airways in 1971 to form British Airways. In the post-war years, the 32 seat Dakota seen in this 1958 picture was the trusty workhorse which replaced the smaller Rapide biplanes on short haul routes. Operating out of Renfrew, the Western Isles service routed via Benbecula and Stornoway to Inverness before returning the same way. As the turn-round at intermediate stops like Benbecula was scheduled for ten minutes, the normal practice was to shut down only the port engine to permit the loading of passengers and baggage.